Dear Cats

The Post Office Letters

Edited by Russell Ash

Illustrated by
Kevin W. Maddison

PAVILION
MICHAEL JOSEPH

First published in Great Britain in 1986 by
Pavilion Books Limited
196 Shaftesbury Avenue, London WC2H 8JL
in association with Michael Joseph Limited
27 Wrights Lane, Kensington, London W8 5TZ

© Text Russell Ash

© Illustrations Kevin W. Maddison

Dear cats: the Post Office letters.
1. Great Britain. *Post Office* 2. Mice——
control——Great Britain——History——
19th century 3.Cats
I. Ash, Russell
628.9′693   TH9041

ISBN 1 85145 085 8

Printed and bound by Butler and Tanner, Somerset

Contents

Introduction

Letters and mail sacks have often been attacked by rats and mice, and for well over a hundred years the British Post Office has found that cats are the most efficient means of combatting this rodent menace.

That, you might suppose, would be the end of the story – except that the Post Office is not quite like most other great British institutions. Every case of mouse attack has been officially reported through the proper channels; every cat that has ever been 'employed' has been the subject of often detailed internal correspondence; and the terms and conditions of employment of each cat have been scrupulously established in memoranda that have winged their way around the Post Office – sometimes up to Postmaster General level. And the result is that the Post Office cat letters form a substantial collection preserved in the Post Office Archives in London.

When I discovered them, several questions occurred to me:

Why on earth should the Post Office not only have employed a veritable army of cats, but considered it important enough to keep and meticulously file correspondence on such a seemingly trivial matter?

Why, over the years (nearly 120 of them), had often

very senior Post Office officials (and even Members of Parliament!) engaged in debate in extended series of letters about the employment of cats as mousers, their rates of pay – allowances for food to supplement their 'mouse diet' – and their welfare, and argued every case in often pedantic detail and in such official language?

Why should personnel from postmen to Postmasters General have felt so strongly about the need for cats in Post Offices in the first place?
As I delved, some of the answers emerged:

In the days when hygiene was not as good as it is today, when perishable foodstuffs were commonly sent through the post and jute sacks were used, cats were employed to catch the mice that ate the mail for which the Post Office was temporarily responsible. Postmen are very conscientious people, and every time a letter was nibbled or a parcel munched, they felt they had somehow failed to maintain the standards the public demanded for the safe transmission of their mail. Traps and poison worked only up to a point; the presence of a cat on the premises was always regarded as the ultimate deterrent.

The officialese was explained by the fact that the Post Office has always been a highly bureaucratic organisation, with a clearly defined hierarchy of personnel and long-established codes of practice. The chains of letters that ultimately allowed (or dis-allowed) a department to maintain a cat are indistinguishable from internal memoranda entitling them to employ extra clerks or sorters – and why not? The fact that the employees in question happened to have four legs and whiskers was irrelevant – the system was the system, and had to be followed. After all, the cats were technically employed by the Government, if only in an advisory capacity. It would be interesting to know what their security rating was, but there is no record of this in the Post Office Archives. Nor is there any record of a cat being asked to sign the Official Secrets Act. Just occasionally, though, there is the barest hint that the writer of a particular official cat letter had his tongue ever so slightly in his cheek.

In the world of bureaucracy, the line between the approved and the absurd is often finely drawn, as many incidents illustrate. During the Second World War, for example, an inveterate American practical joker called Hugh Troy found himself serving in the army, where he was responsible for filling out all sorts of ludicrous forms. In an inventive moment, he drafted and printed multiple copies of a Flypaper Report, on which he noted precisely how many flies had been caught on every flypaper, duly sending the completed forms to the Pentagon. It wasn't long before the Flypaper Report became standard army issue, with serious flak resulting for any officer who did not ensure his reports were sent in regularly. The fact that no one really wanted to know how many flies had been caught was almost incidental to the requirement that

the form should be filled in.

Hugh Troy's humour was deliberate; that of the Post Office cat letters is mostly of the unintentional kind and comes about because, although the British Post Office is perhaps not quite so entangled in its own red tape as the U.S. army, there has nevertheless always been a correct procedure for everything – including something as seemingly unimportant as the place of Official Cats. Though to an outsider the result may seem sometimes to verge on the whimsical, within the organisation cats were treated very seriously: Heaven help any Postmaster who took a cat on to his payroll without first obtaining permission to do so and having its allowance sanctioned through the proper channels. A further extension of this is the use of precedents: once an allowance was officially granted, it became the prevailing rate in every Post Office, to be changed only after much pressure.

It is quite obvious too that where cats are concerned, postmen are complete softies. Even when they weren't really essential, every attempt to oust cats from the establishment has been resisted, and over a century of battles have been fought to ensure that the cats have got a square deal as far as their pay and conditions are concerned. Threats such as redundancy, the dilution of their milk, the withdrawal of part of their emoluments to create mousing incentives and other periodic petty-minded anti-cat manoeuvres have been greeted with such howls of protest that on virtually every occasion, however elevated he might be, its instigator has had to withdraw his proposals.

The letters are not without their historical interest in the quirky slant they put on Victorian officialdom and for their revelations of the economics of bygone periods (some not so long ago); 'a shilling a week and all the mice you can catch' was for several decades the standard rate of pay. Especially after the First World War, many women were employed in the Post Office, and a number of the cat letters throw some oblique light on their role. Also, in our telephone age, the elegance of many of the earlier letters is particularly noteworthy – but so too, surprisingly, is the speed of communication: in the nineteenth century, letters were often posted, received and replied to all on the same day! And whatever happened to such services as the 9.00 p.m. collection referred to in one series of letters?

Ultimately, whether you find the Post Office cat letters amusing or revealing, whether they simply reinforce your beliefs about British eccentricity or your worst anarchist prejudices about the absurdity of officialdom, this collection shows one important thing: that however huge a corporation like the Post Office may be, it has always found the time and has always been sufficiently tender-hearted to care for its cats. Personally, I find that immensely reassuring.

RUSSELL ASH

Notes

The letters that follow span the period from 1868 to the present and are arranged chronologically. The total Post Office Archives collection is considerable, and this selection represents only those that throw light on some new development in the story of the Post Office cats.

Especially in the earlier years, the most common procedure was for internal correspondence in the Post Office to be written in the form of an ever-expanding file: partly in the interests of paper economy, the sender of the first letter in a series would be replied to on the bottom of his letter, or on a new sheet of paper attached to the first, and so on. The complete file would ricochet backwards and forwards as questions were asked and the information was supplied, steadily gaining bulk until a conclusion was reached. This explains why the letters have survived and have ended up in the Post Office Archives as remarkably complete groups and in precise date order, and also why it was impossible for letters to cross in the post. Each file would have a 'Registered Papers' number, and senders and recipients would record the essential details of their letters in their personal daybooks; they could, of course, recall the whole file from the system if they needed to consult it.

Younger readers may perhaps need to be told that until 1971 British currency was based on a £ consisting of 20 shillings or 240 pence. One shilling – the long-prevailing weekly pay rate that is the subject of so much argument in the pages that follow – was thus equivalent to 5p.

Until the creation of British Telecom in 1981 the telephone system was controlled by the Post Office, which explains why some of the letters refer to telephone exchanges.

The text of the letters is precise, except that grammatical and spelling errors have been corrected throughout. The ellipsis ... indicates the omission of detail that is irrelevant to Post Office cats, and the square brackets denote my additions.

'How do the Cats get on?'

The First Official Post Office Cats

In the late summer of 1868, a series of internal letters, now filed away in the Post Office Archives as 'Minute No: 88560: Cats: Subsistence Allowance', began a story that has continued until the present day. Concerned by the damage being caused by a plague of mice at the London Money Order Office, Frederic Rowland Jackson, the Controller of the Office, was inspired to suggest to his superior that they should add three cats to the payroll. There had undoubtedly been cats in Post Offices before, but Mr. Jackson was the first to propose their official appointment:

23 September 1868
The Controller, Money Order Office, London
to the Secretary of the Post Office

I beg to report that very serious destruction and mutilation of the paid Money Orders stowed in the Registration Lockers of this Department has been brought about by mice: traps and other means have to no purpose been used for the riddance of these vermin, and I beg to state that I have requested the resident porter, [James] Tye, to procure three cats for the purpose, and for the support of which he will be reimbursed. I understand that 1½d per day is usually allowed at the

---

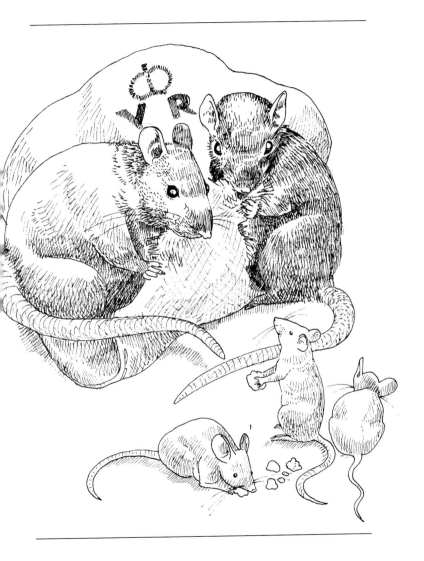

[British] Museum and other places of the kind for each cat kept, and I propose that Tye should be allowed 2/- per week for the keep and care of these cats, which, if approved, can be defrayed by the surplus cash arising from money left at the windows of this department and unclaimed ...

The Secretary received this missive and responded the same day:

23 September 1868
The Secretary of the Post Office
to the Controller, Money Order Office, London

Three cats may be allowed on probation. They must undergo a test examination and should, I think, be females. It is important that the cats be not overfed and I cannot allow more than 1/- a week for their support. They must depend on the mice for the remainder of their emoluments and if the mice be not reduced in number in six months a further portion of the allowance must be stopped. Can any statistics as to mice be furnished from time to time?

24 September 1868
The Controller, Money Order Office, London
to the Secretary of the Post Office

These directions have been communicated to Tye who will no doubt find means to inform the cats upon what terms they are to be employed and what is expected of them. As the destruction of Money Orders is a serious matter, it is to be hoped that the cat movement will be successful.

And so the first Post Office cats started work. On 5 May of the following year, the Controller wrote to the Secretary again with a detailed account of the expenditure on cat food up to the end of 1868. This prompted the Secretary to enquire after the cats:

6 May 1869
The Secretary of the Post Office
to the Controller, Money Order Office, London

How do the cats get on? Is it not time a report were made?

7 May 1869
The Controller, Money Order Office, London
to the Secretary of the Post Office

With reference to this inquiry after the cats by the
Secretary, I am enabled to report that, whether influenced
by the Secretary's caution that they would under certain
contingencies have diminished rations, or by a laudable
zeal for the Service and their own characters, cannot be
clearly made out, but it is certain that the Cat System
has answered exceedingly well and that the cats have
done their duty very efficiently, except as respects one
point of the Secretary's order [that they should be female]
which implied a probable increase in that portion of the
Establishment.

On 8 May, in a note to the Receiver and Accountant General, the Secretary hinted that he '... will consider the propriety of appointing a Committee of Inspection' to examine the 'Cat System', and duly wrote again to the Controller:

11 May 1869
The Secretary of the Post Office
to the Controller, Money Order Office, London

In the event of a Committee of Inspection being appointed, I would suggest that Tye's evidence should be taken as to the test examination. I understand he can explain the reason why the cats have not acted up to orders in the matter of increasing the Establishment?

12 May 1869
The Controller, Money Order Office, London
to the Secretary of the Post Office

A very valuable suggestion which shall not be lost sight of.

There was a lull in the cat correspondence until 1873, when the Southampton Postmaster, George Pellatt, wrote to Mr. Good, the regional Surveyor:

**22 April 1873
The Postmaster, Southampton
to the Surveyor**

Our sack store where the outward Australian mail is kept has become infested with rats and they have begun to injure the correspondence. The Dock Authorities have been spoken to and they state that a cat must be kept in the store. This will be attended with a slight expense and I submit that our Foreign Mail Guard, [James] Wadman, who is stationed here, and who attends to the store, may have a small allowance granted him to pay the expense.

**23 April 1873
The Surveyor
to the Postmaster, Southampton**

What amount will be sufficient to cover the expenses?

17 May 1873
The Surveyor, Southampton
to the Secretary of the Post Office

I have instructed the Postmaster accordingly, and will
make the amount as small as possible; but Mr. Wadman,
the Guard, whose duty it will be to look after the cat,
argues that such a sum as 6d or 9d per week would be
quite insufficient. He says no nourishment whatever can
be derived from rats which reside in the Post Office Store
Room; that picking such rats, fed as they are upon nothing
but mail bags, is no better than picking oakum [rope
fibre]; besides, he very properly points out, that the wear
and tear of shoe leather in going to and fro will cost at
least one fourth of the proposed allowance, and that
whatever small balance there may be left over after
paying these expenses will not be more than sufficient to
compensate him for the loss of dignity in carrying the
cats' food through the streets in Her Majesty's uniform.

*This new request led the Secretary to enquire about the
original complement of cats at the Money Order Office:*

22 May 1873
The Secretary of the Post Office
to the Controller, Money Order Office, London

Has the allowance of 1/- a week for the keep of three cats
in the Money Order Office proved sufficient?

26 May 1873
The Controller, Money Order Office, London
to the Secretary of the Post Office

The allowance of 1/- per week is insufficient to maintain three cats. The cost of the meat alone is 1/- per week and Mrs. Tye, the House Porter's wife, expends about 8d weekly out of her private purse to provide them with milk. I cannot recommend any reduction in the staff of cats as their duties have much increased since the Telegraph Clerks have been here – one cat bringing as many as twelve mice from the top of the building into the kitchen during the evening – I may add that the mice of the town are rather dainty feeders, very different from the rats of Southampton: instead of mail bags they live upon the choice morsels that escape from the Telegraph Clerks' lunches. Under the circumstances ... I submit that the allowance has [to be increased by] 6d per week.

This correspondence was sent to Southampton as evidence of the standard rate of pay:

Undated
The Secretary of the Post Office
to the Postmaster, Southampton

It will be seen from the accompanying that three cats are on the Establishment of the London Money Order Office, and that for the subsistence of all three only 1/- a week has hitherto been allowed. Although this is found to be not quite sufficient, all the increase asked for is 6d, making a total of 1/6d a week for the three animals.

Money Order mice are probably nicer and more tempting feeding than Southampton rats, but notwithstanding any difference in this respect, the Secretary would be quite unable to authorise more than 1/- at the very outside for the Southampton Cat.

Eventually, after protracted negotiations, a pay rate for the Southampton Cat was established, but the Secretary then received the following note:

16 August 1873
The Postmaster, Southampton
to the Secretary of the Post Office

The allowance authorised in the enclosed papers will not be required. The store has been boarded up, and as the floor is paved it is almost impossible for any rat, however clever he or she may be, to gain an entrance. The great 'cat case' is therefore at an end.

But if the Southampton Postmaster and the dignity-conscious Wadman had abandoned their 'cat case', the Money Order Office had won theirs, the allowance being increased by 6d per week, and on 6 September the Controller thanked the Secretary on Mrs. Tye's behalf – asking too if it could be backdated to 1 January, which was approved.

In the Post Office Archives there is even one of porter Tye's accounts for cat food, showing that three cats were still on the staff seven years after they were first appointed. Dated 14 April 1875, it reads:

> An Account of the allowance due to J.E. Tye, the Houseporter at the Money Order Office, for the keep of 3 cats during the quarter ended 31st March 1875:
> From 1 January to 3 March 75
> 13 weeks @ 1/6d a week   19s 6d.

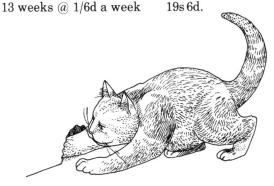

In April 1875, Post Office accountants looked into the question of allowances for cats, complaining that they were evidently too fastidious to be '. . . satisfied with mouse diet', and suggesting that '. . . trial be made of some mechanical contrivances' (i.e. mouse traps), with the alarming comment that '. . . if this proves successful the cats may be pensioned'. This was not the last attempt to make Post Office cats redundant – but little more was heard of the 'mechanical contrivances'.

A typical request of the 1870s – which was immediately approved – was:

20 February 1877
The Post Office Engineer, Nottingham
to the Secretary of the Post Office

Owing to the damage done in Nottingham Depot Stores by rats and mice I have given the storeman instructions to provide two cats. This has been done and I attach an account for their food and care at 6d per week which I ask authority to claim, and also to continue to charge so long as it may be found necessary to do so.

Cats were appointed at Post Offices throughout the 1870s and 1880s. There are records of one joining the staff at the St. Paul's Churchyard, London, Post Office in July 1886, and in December of the same year the Secretary of the Post Office must have been somewhat surprised to receive in his post a box of wedding cake that had been attacked by mice at Deptford Post Office, with a plea for some protection against similar depredations. Several letters were exchanged before the obvious remedy in the form of a cat was suggested and soon appointed – on an annual salary of 15/-. In 1887 more cats were added to the staff at Newgate Street, Fore Street and elsewhere in the London Postal Region.

In 1889 two particularly severe – and somewhat bizarre – outbreaks of metal-devouring super-mice occurred in London, and cats were called in to remedy the situation:

17 June 1889
**The Divisional Officer, Gloucester Road Post Office
   Factory**
to the Controller of Telegraph Stores

Until quite recently we had a number of cats at the
Factory premises which belonged to different men who
fed them, but recently from one cause or another these
cats have disappeared and I find that many of our stores,
particularly bright steel goods[!] and cotton goods are
being very severely damaged by mice. It is therefore very
essential that we should obtain two cats and keep them
about the buildings, and as these cats will have to be
partially fed by the Department, I would ask authority to
charge 2/- fortnightly for the cost of their food. Of course,
this amount will not entirely keep the cats but they are
sure to get some food given them by the men. As it would
be very inconvenient to charge for every ½d or 1d spent
on milk or cats' meat, I would suggest that the most
convenient way of dealing with the matter would be to
hand one of the men 1/- weekly and obtain his receipt
and to hold him responsible for the cats' being fed.

20 June 1889
The Controller of Telegraph Stores
**to the Divisional Officer, Gloucester Road Post Office
   Factory**

Approved.

After consulting Wadman, the Postmaster informed the Surveyor, who wrote to the Secretary:

26 April 1873
The Surveyor
to the Secretary of the Post Office

I beg to submit that an allowance of 1/9d a week will be allowed for the keep of a cat in the store house for the mail at the Docks at Southampton.

28 April 1873
The Secretary of the Post Office
to the Surveyor

This seems a good deal to pay for a cat who is to do much in the 'rat killing' way. In London from 6d to 9d a week is believed to be the usual allowance for a cat's board and wages, varying accordingly to the supply of rats or mice. Is there any reason why more should be paid at Southampton?

24 October 1889
The Controller of Post Office Stores
to the Secretary of the Post Office

Considerable damage is caused to the Gutta Percha wire
which is stored at Mount Pleasant by mice, and it has
occurred to me that most, if not all of this damage, might
be avoided if we maintained a couple of cats on the
premises as at Gloucester Road. I shall therefore be glad
if you will be so good as to obtain authority for the
maintenance of two cats at Mount Pleasant at the rate of
2/- each fortnight (i.e.: 1/- for each cat) and permit me to
claim this amount under 'Incidentals' in the fortnightly
accounts in a similar manner to the arrangement
authorised (in Registered Papers 183314/89) in respect of
the cats maintained at Gloucester Road.

*This was approved on 29 October, and nothing more was
heard of the metal-munching mice.*

'Would a Cat be Desirable?'

Post Office Cats of the 1890s

Leicester Journal 28 November 1890

NATURAL HISTORY IN THE POST OFFICE

The officials at the Leicester Post Office have been studying zoology in a way that is charming – to an outsider. The other day £3 worth of stamps were 'missing'. They were what is known as Civil Service stamps, and worth from 5s to £1 each. The clerks in charge were questioned, but nothing could be elicited from them. Then the drawer where the stamps had been kept was reinstated, and circumstantial evidence was found that seemed to connect some mice with the offence. The way of the sinners was traced through a groove in the anatomy of the office counter, and in another drawer, yards away, further evidence was found – this time in the form of nibbled fragments of the Sovereign's visage. A mouse was, in fact, discovered in the very act of 'getting outside' a five shillings' worth stamp. History does not say precisely what became of these particular convicts. Perhaps they have been transported for life, for we are confidently informed that they will never offend again.

They deserved it, for £4 worth of stamps were missed not long ago, which were supposed to have gone through a little of their handiwork. Of course, as these stamps were never sold to the public, their selling value in money need not necessarily be lost. An application on the subject has been made to the General Post Office.

14 June 1892
E. Topliss, Storekeeper, Leicester Post Office
to T. Phillipson, Postmaster

I beg to state that a large number of forms and documents
having been damaged, and in many instances completely
destroyed by mice at this Office, it is absolutely necessary
to always have a cat on the premises. The cat, however,
is not sufficiently fed, for the officers do not always
remember to bring milk to the Office, therefore I shall be
very glad if you will kindly apply for an Allowance of 1d
per day for the maintenance of the animal.

I have attached a newspaper cutting from the *Leicester
Journal*, dated 28 November 1890, referring to loss and
damage of stamps by mice.

About two years since, when two Judicature Fee
Stamps, value £2 each, were missing, the Clerks who had
charge of the Inland Revenue Stamps were called upon
to pay the amount. The £4, however, was refunded when
another case occurred which clearly showed that the mice
had carried £3 worth of stamps away.

16 June 1892
The Postmaster, Leicester
to the Surveyor

Submitted. So many mice are overrunning these premises
and their depredations are so annoying – and in some
cases serious – that it is really necessary to maintain a
cat in this building.

I should therefore be glad if an allowance of (say) £2 a
year could be given for procuring food for this animal.

18 June 1892
The Surveyor
to the Postmaster, Leicester

At Nottingham an allowance of 1/- a week (£2.12s a year)
is made to the Postmaster for the maintenance of <u>2</u> cats.
I think similar arrangement should be made at Leicester.
Do you agree?

22 June 1892
The Postmaster, Leicester
to the Surveyor

Yes, two cats would probably answer better than one,
and, with the scraps of bread and meat which they would
pick up on the premises, an allowance of 1/- a week for
the maintenance of two animals would doubtless suffice.

Such applications became virtually routine in the 1890s, and many letters exist along the following lines:

4 August 1892
The Registrar
to the Secretary of the Post Office

I beg to report that the Registry room at Throgmorton Avenue is much infested with mice and the books there have already sustained some damage. I should be glad, therefore, if an allowance of 6d per week for the maintenance of a cat could be authorised.

5 August 1892
The Secretary of the Post Office
to the Registrar

Approved.

Not only were letters, mailbags, stamps and various documents suffering from rodent damage, but – as at Deptford in 1886 – food, particularly wedding cake, sent through the post, was vulnerable:

8 November 1898
George Andrews, Postmaster, Liskeard, Cornwall
to B.W. Seton, Surveyor, South Western District

Two cases have recently occurred of letter bags being eaten into by rats and some of the contents (two packets of bridecake and a pastry) destroyed.

The rats come from the adjoining premises, a bakery

and a stable, through a lath and plaster wall, to the basement and thence by the hot water pipes to the sorting-room.

I have directed the bags to be placed on the opening-out table during the night, but consider something should be done to entrap or poison these vermin. Submitted for instructions.

9 November 1898
The Surveyor
to the Postmaster, Liskeard

You may buy some rat poison, or a rat trap. Would a cat be desirable?

7 December 1898
The Surveyor
to the Secretary of the Post Office

Poison has been used and a rat trap borrowed. A few rats have been caught in the trap and some destroyed by the poison, but the vermin seem to know the trap now, and won't touch the poison. Several parcels, such as pork, partridge and cake have been eaten into, and three bags injured. Under the circumstances it is considered a cat would be desirable. I should also like to have tin placed around the hot water pipes in two places, viz.: where the pipes come through the flooring into the public office, and where the pipes pass through the partition into the sorting office – it is thought that if these openings were closed the rats would be unable to get into the sorting office, and the expense would be trivial.

Great care is taken every night to place all parcels containing food on the highest benches, but the vermin manage to reach them.

The bill for the rat poison is submitted.

9 December 1898
The Surveyor
to the Postmaster, Liskeard

The bill for the rat poison is certified.

I will be glad if you will submit an estimate for the work you consider necessary.

I assume you can get a cat without difficulty and expense. Would 6d a week suffice for its maintenance?

The rat problem was now getting urgent: Christmas was coming, and the amount of food parcels being sent through the mail was increasing.

10 December 1898
The Postmaster, Liskeard
to the Surveyor

The ironmonger considers tin could be easily bent, and recommends iron – the estimate for this would be 6/- – if approved the rats would be unable to find access to the sorting office and I should be glad of this protection before Christmas.

A cat could be obtained, and it is thought 6d a week would suffice for its maintenance.

FORE STREET, LISKEARD
Dr. to B. STRONG
General Furnishing Ironmonger, Plumber,
Bell Hanger, Gas Fitter, &c.
Fenders, Fire Irons, Cooking Stoves,
Iron Bedsteads, Cutlery, &c.
All kinds of burning oils, lamps, &c.

Estimate for supplying and fixing galvanised sheet iron around hot water pipes to prevent rats from getting into the offices.

Viz. 6s 0d.

13 December 1898
The Surveyor
to the Postmaster, Liskeard

The annexed estimate may be accepted.

A cat may be obtained forthwith, and on the return of these papers Secretary's authority shall be sought for the maintenance allowance. Sometimes cats prove as aggressive as rats to game, etc., and care must be taken to keep such parcels out of its reach.

18 December 1898
The Postmaster, Liskeard
to the Surveyor

The work has been duly carried out and the tradesman's bill is submitted. It is considered impossible for the rats to gain admittance to the sorting office, unless the door is carelessly left open.

A fair size kitten was obtained last Saturday, and every care shall be taken to secure it downstairs prior to the office being closed.

An allowance of 6d a week was immediately granted for the Liskeard cat.

In the same year, another series of letters began when the Comptroller and Accountant General questioned why the pay of cats earlier employed at Manchester should be regarded as 'Incidents' rather than wages paid to permanent members of staff, who were thus part of the 'Establishment':

18 November 1898
The Comptroller and Accountant General
to H. Harley, Postmaster, Manchester

It is observed that claims are periodically made on 'Incidents' for the cost of food for the cats. As this expenditure seems to be permanently required, will you be good enough to state whether you see any reason why it should not be placed on the Establishment?

17 December 1898
The Postmaster, Manchester
to the Comptroller and Accountant General

An expenditure of 1d a day at the Head Office and 2d a day at the Parcel Post, or 1/9 weekly, is necessary for the cost of food for cats and I see no reason why the amount should not be claimed on the Establishment.

19 December 1898
The Comptroller and Accountant General
to the Secretary of the Post Office

If approved by the Secretary, the amount will be transferred to the Establishment, and Treasury authority is sought in the usual way.

21 December 1898
The Secretary of the Post Office
to the Postmaster, Manchester

Is special provision for the keep of cats really necessary? Could not daily meals be provided from the Refreshment Room waste for all the office cats?

27 January 1899
The Postmaster, Manchester
to the Secretary of the Post Office

An expenditure for the keep of cats is necessary. The cats at the Head Office, Manchester, are fed from the

Refreshment Room waste, and I can arrange for the cats at the Parcel Post Branch to be fed in a similar way.

It will still, however, be necessary to incur an expenditure of 1/2d a week for milk.

30 January 1899
The Secretary of the Post Office
to the Secretary, Buildings Branch

Is 1d a day allowed for each cat in the G.P.O. Buildings?

3 February 1899
The Secretary, Buildings Branch
to the Secretary of the Post Office

The usual allowance for a cat is 6d a week ...

6 February 1899
The Secretary of the Post Office
to the Postmaster, Manchester

The usual allowance appears to be 6d and an allowance of 1/- (which should be an Establishment payment) may therefore perhaps suffice in this case.

25 February 1899
The Postmaster, Manchester
to the Secretary of the Post Office

Noted. The alteration took effect on the 12th instant.

'Are Yours Necessary?'

Edwardian Post Office Cats

The coming of the twentieth century prompted a mood of change in the Post Office, and some of the first questions about the cats' real value were asked. Queen Victoria died on 22 January 1901. The Secretary's letters of this year were therefore black-edged:

24 October 1901
The Secretary of the Post Office
to the Registrar

I find that you have two cats on the Establishment at 6d a week each. As we now pay Snow [a caretaker] to keep your rooms free of mice, amongst other things, the question arises whether the cats might not be abolished.

By whom is the allowance expended?

24 October 1901
The Registrar
to the Secretary of the Post Office

The allowances were for a cat at Throgmorton Street and one in G.P.O. West. On the removal to this building the cats were dispensed with. The allowances are therefore not needed now.

This inspired the Secretary to broaden his enquiry about Post Office cats:

25 October 1901
The Secretary of the Post Office
to the Comptroller and Accountant General

Will the Comptroller and Accountant General be good enough to say which of the allowances for cats are still being drawn?

7 November 1901
The Comptroller and Accountant General
to the Secretary of the Post Office

The following allowances are still being claimed:

25–27 Newgate Street	6d a week
Postal Stores Department	1/- a week
Savings Bank Department	1/3d a week

23 December 1901
The Secretary of the Post Office
to the Controller, Postal Stores Department

Do you really want this still?

3 January 1902
The Controller, Postal Stores Department
to the Secretary of the Post Office

It is most important that the allowance should continue. Recently, when one of the cats was killed by a lift, the Depot to which it belonged was over-run with mice, until a fresh cat was obtained.

4 January 1902
The Secretary of the Post Office
to the Controller, Savings Bank Department

Are yours necessary?

9 January 1902
The Controller, Savings Bank Department
to the Secretary of the Post Office

I think the allowance should be continued. Official Papers and documents have, from time to time, been partially destroyed by mice, and I fear that if any of the precautions which are now taken to keep down the ravages are relaxed, serious damage may result.

The threat was averted – but was to raise its head on several subsequent occasions. The only staff reduction occurred at Leicester, where two cats had been taken on in 1892:

8 November 1907
The Postmaster, Leicester
to the Surveyor

The improved arrangements in this office render unnecessary the provision of more than one cat to cope with any mice that may find their way into the bag room, or any other place where mice are likely to do damage, and I recommend, therefore, that the allowance be reduced accordingly fom 1/- to 6d a week.

War and Puss

Post Office Cats in the First World War

The First World War broke out on 28 July 1914. In the Post Office, it was business as usual:

23 October 1914
**The Assistant Supervisor, 21 Regent Street Branch
 Office**
to the Postmaster

The enclosed parcel [addressed to Miss G. Stevens, Students Hostel, 12 Picardy Place, Edinburgh] was accepted after the 9 p.m. collection last night and retained until this morning locked up in [a] parcel receptacle after the usual practice. This morning it was found to have been attacked by mice. There are mice in the office. Traps have been used [but] it is thought that a cat would be more efficacious [and] one will be provided this week.

It is presumed that 7d a week will be allowed for keep.

23 October 1914
The Postmaster
to the Controller, London Postal Service

Submitted for authority to expend 6d per week for a cat at the 21 Regent Street Branch Office.

4 November 1914
The Controller, London Postal Service
to the Secretary of the Post Office

Re: Regent Street Branch Office
Authority can perhaps be given for the maintenance of a
cat, at a cost of 7d a week, at the office in question.

The Secretary may be disposed to give power to deal
with applications of this kind, in which care would be
taken to see that expense was only authorised where
really necessary and that it was ceased when no longer
really required.

9 November 1914
The Secretary of the Post Office
to the Controller, London Postal Service

Authority is given for an expenditure of 7d per week on the maintenance of the cat.

The question of delegation of authority will be considered on the return of the papers.

1 December 1914
The Secretary of the Post Office
to the Comptroller and Accountant General

Does the Comptroller and Accountant General see any objection to the delegation to Surveyors, etc. of authority to incur expenditure not exceeding 1d per diem per cat on the maintenance of cats?

11 December 1914
The Comptroller and Accountant General
to the Secretary of the Post Office

No objection is seen.

22 February 1915
Memorandum by the Controller

It appears that the existing cat allowances in London
Postal Service are 12 in number, viz.:

  7 South Western District
  3 North Western District
  2 South Eastern District

*Exchanges of letters addressed to or signed by 'the
Secretary' or 'the Controller' were, in fact, very frequently
dealt with by clerical assistants. On this occasion, however,
there is no doubting the personal involvement of these two
very senior officials:*

23 February 1915
Ivor Richards, Controller of the Post Office
to Sir Robert Bruce, Secretary of the Post Office

Dear Bruce,
I don't know whether you have seen these papers.
Personally I doubt the necessity, in the case of a Branch
Office at any rate, of these more or less permanent
allowances.

The temporary services of a cat – with a look around
by the Clerk of the Works to see that holes in floors, etc,
are stopped up – would probably meet the case in most
instances. (I don't know why South West should be so
particularly fond of such allowances.)

Applications from the Provinces for the grant of such
allowances are comparatively rare, and we have had no
suggestion for a general authority, and I think that idea
might wait.
Yours very truly,
Ivor Richards

*On the same day the Controller launched a fact-finding
enquiry:*

23 February 1915
The Controller of the Post Office
to the Postmaster, South Western District

Would you please say at what offices in your District cats
are at present maintained, and whether you consider it
really necessary to continue to keep the animals at those
offices?

25 February 1915
The Postmaster, South Western District
to the Controller of the Post Office

As follows:

South West District Office:	7d weekly
Charles Street:	"
Churton Street:	"
Knightsbridge:	"
Parliament Street:	"
21 Regent Street:	"
Sloane Square:	6d weekly

In view of the very small expense incurred it seems hardly
worth while to get rid of the animals. Possibly they do
not consume many mice or serve any other useful purpose
but their presence in the buildings probably prevents the
entry or increase of vermin.

25 February 1915
The Controller of the Post Office
to the Postmaster, North Western District

Would you please say at what offices in your District cats
are at present maintained, and whether you consider it
really necessary to continue to keep the animals at those
offices?

17 March 1915
The Postmaster, North Western District
to the Controller of the Post Office

Cats are maintained in this District as follows:

N.W. Parcel Office:	7d weekly
Camden Road Branch Office:	"
Hampstead Green Branch Office:	"

I concur with the views expressed by the Postmaster South West District Office.

17 March 1915
The Controller of the Post Office
to the Postmaster, South Eastern District

Would you please say at what offices in your District cats are at present maintained, and whether you consider it really necessary to continue to keep the animals at those offices?

23 March 1915
The Postmaster, South Eastern District
to the Controller of the Post Office

A cat is maintained at the Borough High Street and at Peckham Branch Offices and it is believed they serve a useful purpose. I therefore am in favour of their retention.

The papers were then forwarded to Sir Robert Bruce.

23 March 1915
Sir Robert Bruce, Secretary of the Post Office
to Ivor Richards, Controller of the Post Office

Dear Richards,

I have looked through these papers.

I do not think that the temporary services of a cat (i.e.: anything under several months) would be sufficient in those instances where the premises concerned have become really verminous, and cat allowances have not usually been authorised until such has been the case. At the same time, I am inclined to think that there may be grounds for dispensing with the services of some of the animals mentioned in the foregoing reports from Postmasters S.W., N.W. and S.E. If you will have the papers recharged to me, I will have inquiries made in that direction.

Yours truly,

Robert Bruce

Sir Robert then evidently made private enquiries, of which there are no records. Two months later he reported again to the Controller:

11 June 1915
Sir Robert Bruce, Secretary of the Post Office
to Ivor Richards, Controller of the Post Office

The question has been pursued with the District
Postmasters concerned, and it is found that they are very
strongly in favour of retention of the cats at the Offices
mentioned. Although holes in the floors are attended to
as soon as they are discovered, it is not found practicable
by this means alone to minimise the nuisance, and the
Postmasters urge that if the cats were withdrawn the
Offices would soon be overrun by mice.

In some cases, the character of the business carried on
next door to the Office contributes to the nuisance.

We might dispense with the cat at Charles Street
Branch Office when we move into the new premises, and
when the second section of the new North Western
District Office is completed the cat at the present North
Western Parcel Office can be got rid of.

14 June 1915
Ivor Richards, Controller of the Post Office
to Sir Robert Bruce, Secretary of the Post Office

Read and noted.

The question of a general authority might stand over
for the present.

18 June 1915   Bruce to Controller

Noted.

As far as can be ascertained, all 12 cats were retained. After these exertions, the Secretary seemed resigned to the idea of cat allowances, as his terse response to an enquiry later in 1915 suggests:

16 October 1915
The Postmaster, Manchester
to the Secretary of the Post Office

Owing to the prevalence of mice at St. Peter's Branch Office, Manchester, it has been found necessary to keep a cat, and I beg leave to ask for authority to commence an allowance of 6d per week for its keep.

22 October 1915
The Secretary of the Post Office
to the Postmaster, Manchester

Authority is given.

During the First World War, cats performed valiant service, as an August 1917 report by the Office of Works on rats and mice in Government buildings exemplified. After considering the problems and dangers of using germ warfare and poisons, it concluded:

The only means left for general use in buildings are cats, traps, and the services of professional rat catchers. As it is practically impossible to obtain the last named so long as the war lasts, the only resources left are the case of cats and traps, and there appears to be no reason to think that if sufficient care and determination are exercised, it will be difficult by using these means to keep down successfully such a pest as is complained of. In the Board's opinion, everything depends on the measures which are taken by Post Office officials on the spot. At a large number of Post Office Buildings in the London area it has been possible to keep down the nuisance mainly by employing cats. Cases in point are the following:

> General Post Office West and Roman Bath Street Buildings
> General Post Office South
> Avenue Telephone Exchange
> The Savings Bank
> London Wall Telephone Exchange
> South Western District Office

At the last named it is gathered that a pest of rats was successfully kept under by the use of cats.

During the War too, food scarcity and rising prices were
beginning to result in frequent complaints that cat
allowances of around 6d a week were inadequate:

15 June 1916
The Superintending Engineer, London Engineering
   District
to the Engineer-in-Chief

Owing to the recent increase in the cost of milk, it will
be necessary to spend an additional 2d per fortnight for
the maintenance of the cat at present kept in the Stores
at Wandsworth. I shall be glad, therefore, if authority to
increase the allowance from 1/- to 1/2d per fortnight may
be given.

16 June 1916
The Engineer-in-Chief
to the Secretary of the Post Office

Submitted. Perhaps the desired authority may be given.

30 June 1916
The Secretary of the Post Office
to the Engineer-in-Chief

On the understanding that the maintenance of a cat at
the Stores is considered essential, authority is given for
an increase of the allowance to 1/2d a fortnight.

5 September 1917
The Postmaster, West Central District Office
to the Secretary of the Post Office

The question of an allowance for the maintenance of a
cat at High Holborn Branch Office has been raised, and
I shall be glad to know whether there is existing authority
under which a Departmental Allowance may be granted
in such cases.

[undated] September 1917
The Secretary of the Post Office
to the Postmaster, West Central District Office

The question of granting such an allowance for the
maintenance of a cat at the High Holborn Branch Office
shall be considered. Perhaps a separate report will be
made on the subject. If the matter has been referred to
in previous papers, doubtless the number will be given.
How was the cat obtained?
How long has it been kept at the Office?
How is it maintained now?

24 September 1917
The Postmaster, West Central District Office
to the Secretary of the Post Office

Arising out of the Secretary's memorandum on the
subject of Rats and Mice in Government Buildings, the
question of an allowance for the maintenance of a cat at
High Holborn Branch Office has arisen. For the past

three and a half years, the services of a cat have been utilised at the High Holborn Branch Office. The premises were overrun with mice in 1913, but the presence of a cat has since successfully kept down the pest. Kittens have been procured without charge by the female cleaner employed at the Office ... The cat has been maintained by scraps from the dinners of the staff, and by milk supplied from the staff's Tea Club. Cats are also kept at Bedford Street and West Strand Branch Offices, and in the event of a maintenance allowance being granted in the case of High Holborn Branch Office, it is probable that applications would be received from the other two offices for similar treatment. It is recommended that an allowance of 7d per week be authorised for maintaining the cat at High Holborn Branch Office. The question as regards the other Branch Offices can be dealt with as it arises ...

6 October 1917
The Secretary of the Post Office
to the Controller, London Postal Service

Authority is given for an allowance of 7d a week for the keep of a cat at the High Holborn Branch Office, West Central, if you are satisfied that sufficient scraps and waste milk, etc. from the meals of the staff are not available for the cat ...

Wartime shortages meant that other, similar applications were treated with circumspection:

14 March 1918
The Postmaster, South Shields
to Mr. A. Mellersh, Surveyor

Owing to complaints from the staff of mice and rats in the office, a cat was obtained four weeks ago with the result that it keeps the office clear of vermin and I shall be glad if an allowance of 9d a week for milk for the cat can be made, as I think it should no longer be left to charity to provide milk.

16 March 1918
The Surveyor
to the Secretary of the Post Office

I know such allowances have been made in the past, and shall be glad of the necessary authority for the proposed allowance if it has not been decided that such allowances can no longer be granted.

[undated] April 1918
The Secretary of the Post Office
to the Surveyor

In view of the necessity for saving all articles of human consumption, the present moment is inopportune for increasing the number of the allowances authorised for the purpose of providing cats with milk, but authority is given in this particular case for the usual allowance of 7d per week if you are quite satisfied of the necessity for maintaining a cat on the Post Office premises at South Shields.

10 May 1918
The Surveyor
to the Secretary of the Post Office

Noted. A cat is very necessary on the premises. Since the cat has been introduced the trouble has disappeared, but it could appear again of the cat were dispensed with.

*In the First World War, there was a large influx of women
into Post Office jobs that were previously dominated by
men. The addition of numbers to the letter prefixes of
London postal areas (E.C., N.W., etc.), which dates from
this time, was introduced because their male employers
regarded them as insufficiently intelligent to comprehend
letter codes alone! But they confounded their male
chauvinist colleagues and rose rapidly to positions of
authority in the service. An application by Camden Road,
London, Branch Office introduces the first female employee
into the cat letters and also provides an interesting glimpse
of rising costs and the prevailing attitudes towards Post
Office cats at the end of the First World War.*

4 May 1918
**Miss Garner, Acting Assistant Supervisor, Camden
 Road Branch Office**
to the Postmaster

I beg to ask if the weekly allowance for the maintenance
of the cat can be increased.

Under present circumstances 7d will not purchase
sufficient milk for a week, and the price of cats' food is
quite as much again as it was when the present allowance
was granted. It is necessary to have a cat on these
premises, otherwise they would be overrun with mice. I
should therefore feel grateful if an extra allowance could
be made.

6 May 1918
The Postmaster
to the Supervisor

Please say what the weekly cost of maintenance should be at present, and how the total is arrived at.

7 May 1918
The Supervisor
to the Postmaster

Sixpence weekly is sufficient for milk now the price is reduced, and for lights [animal lungs], on which the cat is fed, 1/- to 1/3d weekly – the quantity supplied by the butcher varying. The Housekeeper would be satisfied if 1/6d weekly could be allowed.

[undated]
The Postmaster
to the Controller, London Postal Service

Submitted for consideration. A further report from the Officer in Charge is attached in which he explains the difficulty in providing for the cat's maintenance under existing conditions. The case calls, I think, for a substantial increase in the allowance but I do not think that an expenditure of as much as 1/6d weekly is justified. I would recommend the payment of 1/- and that the cat be induced, by abstinence if necessary, to drink diluted milk.

10 May 1918
The Postmaster
to the Supervisor

Is there no alternative to feeding the cat on lights? They are known to be expensive and an increase of the allowance from 7d to 1/6d a week is rather difficult to justify if other food is obtainable at a lower rate. Is the milk diluted before it is given to the cat?

11 May 1918
The Supervisor
to the Postmaster

There seems to be no other food; ordinary cats' meat is now 8d per lb and would be more expensive than lights. The milk is not diluted as the cat, always having been used to milk alone, will not drink milk and water. 7d per week would never have been sufficient to keep a cat, had

there not been a fair amount of food left from the dinner table to help. Since the meat rationing nothing is left and all food for the cat has to be purchased.

The situation at Camden Road was drawn to the attention of the Controller of the London Postal Service:

13 June 1918
The Controller, London Postal Service
to the Postmaster

Are you satisfied that mice are still prevalent at Camden Road Branch Office or that they would become prevalent if the cat were withdrawn? It is not usual, it is thought, to feed a cat that is kept for killing mice only, not as a pet, on meat and it is gathered that this is your view and that you recommend an increase in the allowance owing to the increased price of milk, but will you please confirm. Can the prices of milk in your district before the War and at present be stated?

5 July 1918
The Postmaster
to the Controller, London Postal Service

It is stated at the Parcel Office that the maintenance of a cat is necessary, and that in view of the present price of cats' meat on which it is fed a little more liberal allowance than is purchasable with the 7d weekly now authorised is desirable. A cat is no longer kept at Hampstead Green Branch Office, the animal formerly maintained there having disappeared, and the need for replacing it not having arisen the allowance has been discontinued. The need for a cat at Camden Road Branch Office seems to be apparent, it being stated that mice are often seen there, and that both there and at the Parcel Office, the cats are known to frequently kill mice. The understanding here is that the 7d a week authorised for cat maintenance was made up of 1d per day, one half of the money being for cats' meat, and the other for milk. The pre-war prices of these commodities were 4d (or less) per lb, and 4d per quart respectively, the present respective prices being 8d per lb and 7d per quart, and on these figures the higher allowance recommended is thought to be fully warranted. A similar higher allowance is recommended for the Parcel Office. As regards feeding a cat, the view here is that it is necessary to give a cat a regular meal daily, leaving it to supplement its rations by destroying mice.

9 July 1918
The Controller, London Postal Service
to the Secretary of the Post Office

... Perhaps the Secretary will give authority for the temporary increase to 1/- of the cat allowances in the North Western Parcel Office and at the Camden Road Branch Office. In the absence of complaints from other Offices, it is presumed that matters are satisfactory there – probably more broken food is available – and there seems no need to increase the cat allowances generally, although the total number in the London Postal Service is not large.

'A Thorough Good Mouser'

Post Office Cats of 1919

For no apparent reason, the year 1919 was The Year of the Cat, as far as applications for Post Office cat allowances were concerned.

Until recently, telephones came under the aegis of the Post Office. In 1919 a notable mouse invasion occurred at London's Telephone House, resulting in a series of internal letters between various officials in the Accountant General's Department:

13 February 1919
Mr. C.E. Boxall
to Mr. Rendell

Cases have come to my notice, during the past few days, of telegrams and papers having been mutilated by mice in our rooms. A few telegrams have been eaten away by mice to such an extent as to be useless. Beyond the inconvenience caused by the mutilation of forms, etc. I have no particular objection, but some of the ladies are rather perturbed. Can anything be done in the matter please?

13 February 1919
Mr. Rendell
to Mr. P. T. Lloyd (Clerk in the Comptroller and
  Accountant General's Office)

Can you suggest anything? How about instituting an office cat?

14 February 1919
Mr. P. T. Lloyd
to Mr. Rendell

We obtained one or two cats in similar circumstances at St. Bride Street by appealing to the staff – you will no doubt remember from Money Order Branch experience that a maintenance allowance can be claimed under Incidental Expenses, the present rate being, I believe, 7d per week (inclusive of War Bonus!). The Stores

Department will also supply you with mousetraps on application through your usual Branch requisition.

14 February 1919
Mr. Rendell
to Mr. Goodman

Perhaps you will make enquiries as to how many rooms are frequented by mice and apply for a sufficient number of traps as a first step.

18 February 1919
Mr. Goodman
to Mr. Rendell

I understand that the number of traps would be too great to be practicable.

19 February 1919
Mr. Rendell
to Mr. P. T. Lloyd

It appears on further enquiry as to the number of traps required, that the mice frequent practically every room in the building. So many traps would be wanted that it would require someone to look after the traps. In the circumstances, at least two cats seem to be necessary, but I am afraid I cannot undertake to supply them or to arrange for their maintenance. There is too much other work to be done in the Foreign Telegrams Branch.

19 February 1919
Mr. P. T. Lloyd
to Mr. Stears

What do you suggest? The cats and traps at an ordinary
Post Office would be looked after by the caretaker or
charwoman, but we do not employ any person of the
former rank and Miss Cobby (the Housekeeper) would
probably object to the assignment of such duties to the
latter. Could not your rat catcher undertake the job?

26 February 1919
Mr. Stears
to Mr. P. T. Lloyd

I am sorry but I cannot depart from our practice which is
that occupants of buildings deal with such troubles as
mice.

26 February 1919
Mr. P. T. Lloyd
to Mr. Grant

Will you please see the attached correspondence
regarding mice at Telephone House. Cats are borne on
the Establishment of local Post Offices, but the
circumstances are rather different in the Accountant
General's Office – there is no official to look after their
welfare. We are certainly maintaining a cat at St. Bride
Street (although one or two fine specimens have been
appropriated – by envious neighbouring furriers' firms

we suspect), but this is probably explained by the fact that the building is occupied solely by female staff. It seems to me that in the case of a Department like ours the Office of Works should assist, but failing that do you think that the Stores Department should be regarded as the experts for mice extermination?

6 March 1919
The Secretary of the Post Office
to the Comptroller and Accountant General

Please see the attached memorandum [the August 1917 Office of Works report]. A cat would probably be the most effective method of getting rid of the mice ...

12 March 1919
The Comptroller and Accountant General
to the Secretary of the Post Office

It has now been possible to arrange locally for the employment of a cat.

In the same year, an outbreak of mice at the Branch Office at 70 Oxford Street, London, led to an exchange of over two dozen letters:

15 May 1919
Miss Whamond, Assistant Supervisor, 70 Oxford
  Street
to the Postmaster

May some steps be taken to destroy the mice which appear to be very numerous at the counter at this office? Last night and the night before serious damage has been done to parcels which were left in the office overnight. The ordinary traps supplied are no use.

16 May 1919
The Postmaster
to Miss Whamond

If the traps were supplied officially, please give the
number of the papers referring. Who attends to the
baiting and setting? Is there any allowance for the work?
What make of trap is being used? Under what
circumstances were parcels detained overnight?

[undated] May 1919
Miss Whamond
to the Postmaster

The traps were supplied officially, but there are no
registered papers referring. One of the staff usually
attends to the baiting, etc. The trap is the ordinary
backbreak make. Parcels are detained overnight
regularly here in large numbers because there is not
sufficient room in the collection carts.

20 May 1919
The Postmaster
to Miss Whamond

Is food left lying about overnight? Are the breadcrumbs
(and waste bread if any) swept up in the Retiring Room
and Messengers' Kitchen immediately after the last tea
reliefs? If not will you please see that this is done
regularly. How many traps are in use? Is the failure due
to the traps not acting or to an insufficient number of
traps?

21 May 1919
Miss Whamond
to the Postmaster

No food is left lying about overnight. Breadcrumbs and
waste bread are cleared away in Retiring Rooms and
Messengers' rooms. There are two or three small traps in
use, but mice never go near them. A different kind of trap
is required and some strong poison to do away with them.

22 May 1919
The Postmaster
to the Clerk of Works

The Clerk of Works will perhaps see whether a remedy
can be applied.

2 June 1919
The Clerk of Works
to the Postmaster

Attention has been given to this matter and all that I can
do has been done to assist you to be rid of the nuisance,
in the matter of stopping holes, runs, etc.

But H.M. Office of Works do not undertake to
exterminate vermin.

6 June 1919
Miss Holland, Assistant Supervisor
to the Postmaster

... The stopping up of the holes has not stopped the nuisance.

11 June 1919
The Postmaster
to the Stores Duty Officer

Can any further steps be taken?

13 June 1919
The Stores Duty Officer
to the Postmaster

I can only suggest mouse traps.

23 June 1919
The Postmaster
to the Controller, London Postal Service

... The difficulty arising from the presence of mice at 70 Oxford Street continues, despite the work which has been done by the Office of Works. A good many parcels containing food, which have had to be left in the Office overnight, have been damaged by mice recently.

Perhaps a cat would be useful, if one can be obtained, and authority for the usual allowance of 1d a day is therefore sought.

27 June 1919
The Controller, London Postal Service
to the Postmaster

Authority given. The amount should be claimed on
Incidents for the time being and a further report will be
called for in two months' time.

1 July 1919
The Postmaster
to the Head Porter

Do you think you could secure a good <u>male</u> cat for 70
Oxford Street Branch Office? You probably see a number
of men who might know of such an animal.

2 July 1919
The Head Porter
to the Assistant Superintendant

I have a thorough good mouser (male cat) on the building
which I believe would give every satisfaction at 70 Oxford
Street.

7 July 1919
The Postmaster
to the Controller, London Postal Service

A cat has been obtained and taken to the Branch Office.

Unfortunately, the 'thorough good mouser' did not stay long:

5 September 1919
Miss Holland
to the Postmaster

I beg to report that the mice are again overrunning the building.

The forms kept in the cupboards are being destroyed and rendered useless through being nibbled by the vermin.

6 September 1919
The Postmaster
to Miss Holland

Have you a cat now? One was authorised ... and sent to you. It was afterwards understood that the cat disappeared and subsequently returned.

9 September 1919
Miss Holland
to the Postmaster

Unfortunately there was no return of the wandering cat.

10 September 1919
The Postmaster
to the Head Porter

Is it possible to obtain a cat? ...

11 September 1919
The Head Porter
to the Assistant Superintendant

Attended to: the new cat was handed over to Miss Holland at 10.30 a.m. this morning.

11 September 1919
The Controller, London Postal Service
to the Postmaster

For further report.

Can the cat be dispensed with or is its retention recommended? In the latter case, please report fully on the point.

12 September 1919
The Postmaster
to Miss Holland

For report. Care will no doubt be taken to retain this cat.
The allowance of 7d a week can again be claimed.

13 September 1919
Miss Holland
to the Postmaster

Every care is being taken to retain the cat, which is
already doing good service. Three mice were caught the
first night. The allowance of 7d will be claimed each week.
I might suggest that with milk at its present price 7d per
week is not sufficient allowance.

15 September 1919
The Postmaster
to Miss Lines, Assistant Supervisor

For further report please.

17 September 1919
Miss Lines
to the Postmaster

The cat is justifying its existence, and its retention is
strongly recommended.

It is thought the allowance should be increased to 1/-
per week, in view of the increased price of milk.

20 September 1919
The Postmaster
to the Controller, London Postal Service

It will be seen from the attached local papers that the cat originally supplied had disappeared with the result that further trouble with the mice arose and another cat had to be obtained. In the circumstances, the retention of the cat is recommended. It is thought that the milk allowance should be increased and perhaps the Controller will agree one quart per week at the current price.

27 September 1919
The Controller, London Postal Service
to the Secretary of the Post Office

It has been found necessary to keep a cat on the premises at 70 Oxford Street Branch Office, for Official purposes. A cat allowance of 6d a week for the maintenance of the cat was authorised in June of this year, but an increase in this allowance is asked for and appears to be necessary. Authority is sought to increase the allowance to 1/- per week.

A weekly cat allowance of 1/- for the Kings Cross Branch Office was authorised in registered papers 73553/19.

Finally, on 2 October 1919, authority was granted for an increase to 1/- a week.

Later in 1919, a particularly alarming outbreak of rats occurred at Bristol:

4 December 1919
District Manager, Bristol Post Office
to the Secretary of the Post Office

I regret to report that the District Office building is still suffering from the prevalence of rats. Only a night or two ago a large rat dropped on the shoulders of one of the female cleaners as she was descending the staircase, which gave her a considerable shock. Rats have been seen recently in the female clerks' cloakroom on the top floor. Rats have been caught in the kitchen on the top floor and the male clerks' retiring room on the second floor. They are also seen in the instrument room and boiler house in the basement. On another occasion, whilst one of the female night staff was resting, in feeling for her bag she put her hand on a rat. I shall be glad if further immediate steps can be taken by the Office of Works to stop the nuisance.

19 January 1920
James Eggar, H.M. Office of Works
to the Secretary of the Post Office

Subject: Bristol. Telephone Exchange Building, Rats in the Telephone District Office.

... The City Engineer places great reliance in cats to keep away vermin, and the Board recommend that the Post Office should keep two official cats on the premises.

If this is done, and the minor arrangement mentioned in the report adhered to, it is thought that all grounds for reasonable complaint will be eliminated.

3 February 1920
The Secretary of the Post Office
to the District Manager

One cat might first be tried as an experiment and an allowance not exceeding 1/- a week for its maintenance is authorised ...

9 February 1920
The District Manager
to the Secretary of the Post Office

Noted. A cat will be tried as suggested ...

The Purring Twenties

Post Office Cats of the Jazz Age

During the 1920s, telephone exchanges continued to succumb to rodent invasions:

1 October 1920
Telephone Supervisor, Torquay Exchange
to Mr. Boulton, Postmaster, Torquay

The Engineers report that rats are making their way through a hole in the wall of the Test Room.

1 October 1920
The Postmaster
to the Surveyor

Submitted. This matter should perhaps be attended to by the Engineering Branch.

15 October 1920
The Surveyor
to the Postmaster

Can you suggest any effective way of exterminating the rats please? Are not the local authority taking action as regards rat killing generally? If so you can perhaps make

---

enquiries and ascertain what actually is done to destroy such vermin. What is the size of the hole?

18 October 1920
The Postmaster
to the Surveyor

So far as the local authorities are concerned there are no arrangements for the destruction of rats ...

Assuming the contractor to the Office of Works were required to stop up the hole, about three inches in diameter, and repair the wall plaster where it has been eaten away, the rodents would probably soon eat through at another point. Stopping the hole and laying down some of the advertised rat killer appears to be the only thing to be done.

20 October 1920
H.W. Austin, the Surveyor, Post Office, Exeter
to the District Surveyor, H.M. Office of Works,
  Bristol

I am informed by the Postmaster that rats have penetrated the wall of the Test Room making a hole about three inches in diameter. I shall be glad to know whether you can take any steps to exterminate the rats as it is feared that if the hole already made were merely filled up they would eat through in other places.

26 October 1920
The District Surveyor, H.M. Office of Works
to the Post Office Surveyor

Referring to your letter of the 20th inst., with reference
to rats, I have given instructions for the rat holes to be
stopped up.

In other buildings under the charge of this Department,
various methods for exterminating the rats have been
adopted, and the most successful appears to be to keep a
powerful cat on the premises.

29 October 1920
The Surveyor
to the Postmaster

... Can you procure a powerful cat?

30 October 1920
The Postmaster
to Miss M.E. Jarvis, Supervisor

Can you make any suggestion as to the proposal to keep
a cat on the premises?

Miss Jarvis was clearly not a cat-lover:

2 November 1920
The Supervisor
to the Postmaster

I do not think the premises are suitable for keeping a cat, and in my opinion filling in the holes would be sufficient.

3 November 1920
The Postmaster
to the Supervisor

In what respect are the premises unsuitable for a cat?

4 November 1920
The Supervisor
to the Postmaster

There are several cats in the neighbourhood who are constantly on these premises and are already a nuisance. If these cats are unable to keep away the rats, I do not think an additional cat would be of use.

5 November 1920
The Postmaster
to the Supervisor

The cats in the neighbourhood probably drive rats to premises unprotected by a cat. If a cat were kept in the

Switch Room, especially during the night, it would have a tendency to frighten away even if it did not actually kill them. Will you therefore please make enquiry with a view to obtaining a strong cat to be kept on the Exchange premises?

20 November 1920
The Supervisor
to the Postmaster

Enquiries have been made and a kitten is being procured for the Exchange.

20 November 1920
The Postmaster
to the Surveyor

Enquiry, with a view to securing a strong cat, has been made unsuccessfully. Even if one were obtained it is questionable whether it would remain in such an inhospitable home as a Telephone Exchange. An endeavour is being made to obtain a good-sized kitten which may perhaps settle at the Exchange.

23 November 1920
The Surveyor
to the Postmaster

Have the rat holes been stopped up, please?

No doubt you will keep the matter under notice and report again, say, in three months' time ... How is the kitten fed?

7 January 1921
The Postmaster
to the Surveyor

The rat holes have been stopped.

The cost of feeding the cat is 1/8d a week. Should the amount be claimed on Incidents, please?

10 January 1921
The Surveyor, Western District
to the Accountant General of the Post Office

May the allowance of 1/8d a week be put on the Establishment without Secretarial authority, please?

14 January 1921
The Accountant General
to the Secretary of the Post Office

So far as can be traced the authority to deal with such cases has not been specifically delegated to Surveyors and perhaps the Secretary will say whether is desired that future cases should be submitted for covering authority. If and when the price of milk, etc. falls it may be possible to effect a reduction in the amount of the allowance, but presumably this point may be left to the discretion of the Surveyor.

20 January 1921
The Secretary of the Post Office
to the Surveyor

The proposed allowance is considered too high. On the average – both in London and the provinces – it is found that an allowance of 1/- per week is sufficient to cover the cost of a cat's food.

This apparently provides for one regular meal daily, leaving the cat to supplement its rations by the destruction of rats; and it is thought that a cat will justify its existence to a greater extent if it is made to depend partly on its own exertions.

Perhaps you will agree that the usual allowance of 1/- per week will suffice in this case.

P.S.: Given a reasonable supply of rats or mice it is not quite clear why an efficient cat should not be entirely self-supporting.

*The Surveyor clearly did not agree with the P.S., alongside
which he added two exclamation marks.*

**1 February 1921
The Surveyor
to the Secretary of the Post Office**

Noted. An allowance of 1/- a week has been sanctioned.

**5 February 1921
The Secretary of the Post Office
to the Accountant General**

As applications for such allowances are comparatively
rare the question of delegation of authority might stand
over for the present. The matter will however be borne in
mind when the question of any further delegation to
Surveyors is being considered.

*This standard 'a shilling a week and all the mice you can
catch' rate was to remain in force for over thirty years,
until 1952 – see page 106.*

12 May 1921
The Postmaster, Leicester
to the Surveyor

It is necessary to maintain a cat at the Postmen's Office,
Campbell Street. One is already in residence but has so
far existed on the charity of the Staff employed at that
Office. I should, therefore, be glad if the present
allowance of 6d per week for maintenance of a cat may
be increased to 1/-. Papers 530112/07 returned herewith
refer.

13 May 1921
The Surveyor
to the Postmaster

Presumably, the allowance of 1/- a week would be for the
maintenance of two cats?

17 May 1921
The Postmaster
to the Surveyor

The increased allowance would provide for two cats – one
at the Head Office and one at the Postmen's Office.

*This was duly granted. Five years later, a similar request
was made:*

23 November 1926
The Sectional Engineer, Leicester
to the Postmaster

It is found necessary to keep a cat in the Store Room
occupied by the Department at Campbell Street to keep
down the mice.

I shall be glad if you will kindly arrange for the usual
allowance to be made.

30 November 1926
The Postmaster
to the Surveyor, North Midlands District

Submitted. An allowance for maintenance of a cat at
Head Office was authorised in papers 530112/07 and was
increased in respect of an additional cat for the Postmen's
Office in papers 87441/21.

The rooms for which the Sectional Engineer requires a
cat are detached from the Postmen's Office and perhaps
authority may be given for the existing allowance of 1/-
to be increased to 1/6d ...

3 December 1926
The Surveyor
to the Secretary of the Post Office

Submitted. Perhaps authority may be given for the
allowance of 1/- authorised in papers 87441/21 to be
increased to 1/6d.

7 December 1926
The Secretary of the Post Office
to the Surveyor

Authority is given. How exactly is the presence of so many mice on the premises accounted for? Is food left about?

17 December 1926
The Surveyor
to the Secretary of the Post Office

Noted.

The premises are adjacent to the L.M. & S. Railway Station where, of course, there is always food and other matter which attracts rats and mice.

The trouble is of long standing and was reported to the Ministry of Agriculture and Fisheries in February 1924. After repairs to drains and sewers were carried out the rats disappeared but mice are still prevalent.

Food is not left about by the staff.

15 September 1925
The Postmaster, St. Tibbs Row Parcel Office,
   Cambridge
to the Surveyor

During the last six months fifteen forms P.66 [damaged parcel reports] have been issued in connexion with parcels thought to have been damaged by mice at St. Tibbs Row P.O. In addition, three claims for compensation have been met, amounting to 16/9d, for damage to parcels containing food. It seems desirable, therefore, that a cat should be kept on the premises for the purpose of destroying the mice, although it is feared that, in the absence of a regular supply of milk and food, she would not stay, but I should be glad if I may be informed, before obtaining a cat, whether authority can be given for an allowance of 6d per week for the maintenance of a cat.

It should perhaps be mentioned that at Leicester an allowance of 1/- per week is in existence for the maintenance of two cats on the Post Office premises ...

21 September 1925
The Secretary of the Post Office
to the Surveyor

Authority is given.

20 January 1928
The Postmaster
to the Surveyor

The cat has been very useful in destroying rats and mice and during the last two years there have been no cases of parcels damaged by vermin at the St. Tibbs Row Parcel Office. Considerable difficulty has, however, been experienced in providing sufficient milk and food for the cat. There is no retiring room at St. Tibbs Row Parcel Office and it has been necessary to collect scraps of food from the retiring rooms at the Head Office and the Telephone Exchange. The amount of such food varies and in order to augment the supply I find that two officers employed at the St. Tibbs Row Parcel Office have regularly purchased food and milk at their own expense, particularly at the weekend when the Parcel Office is closed from midnight Saturday to 7.00 a.m. Monday. In the circumstances, I shall be glad if the maintenance allowance may be increased from 6d to 1/- a week.

This request was granted on 31 January.

'You Dirty Rats!'

Post Office Cats of the 1930s and 1940s

---

*In the 1920s and into the 1930s, cats were employed at
many Post Offices, including Earls Court, Baker Street,
Grosvenor Street and Holloway in London and in
Manchester. The standard rate of 1/- a week was
customarily authorised. In January 1930, the Stores
Department asked the Accountant General '... to note that
an additional cat has been added to the strength of the
Engineering Depot'. Cats were employed at the Post Office
Stores Mechanical Transport Section, Dudley House, at 1/-
a week and at Coventry at a cut-price 6d a week.*

24 March 1932
The Surveyor, North Wales District
to the Secretary of the Post Office

Various kinds of vermin killer supplied by the local
authority have been used to exterminate the mice which
overrun the Chester Head Post Office retiring rooms but
the result has not proved satisfactory. This has been
specially noticeable in the Females' Retiring Room,
where the mice on occasions have interfered with the
food brought in by members of the staff, and it is feared
that, unless the pest is overcome, serious complaints will
be received.

It is considered that the only effective way of ridding the premises of the nuisance is to keep a cat on the building and authority is sought to expend 6d a week for the cat's maintenance.

1 April 1932
The Secretary of the Post Office
to the Surveyor, North Wales District

Approved.

In 1939, while war clouds loomed, an increased cat allowance was requested and granted at Eastbourne, and another at Warwick, where chocolate-loving mice were wreaking havoc:

25 January 1939
The Head Postmaster, Warwick & Leamington Spa
to the Surveyor

Some time ago there were numerous well-founded complaints at this office of damage to 'gift packets' of chocolate posted by Messrs. Cadbury of Bournville, Birmingham, contained in bags received overnight for delivery next morning. The damage was clearly done by mice and it became necessary to stack the packets on a platform to keep them out of reach. The Office of Works supplied an adhesive to spread on loose boards to catch the mice. This was effective but the mice died squealing, and at the request of the staff the use of this method was discontinued. Shortly afterwards a cat was introduced into the office and the trouble ceased and has not reappeared. It is not known where the cat came from, and no specific authority was given to keep it in the Office. The staff feed it at their own expense, and the Staff Side have now asked that an official allowance for its food should be authorised. They suggest 1/- a week and assure me that there are precedent cases at other offices. I think myself that some such expenditure would be well warranted, not only in view of the cat's efficiency, but as a kindly and humane gesture on the part of the Department. If there are official objections or difficulties about authorising an 'allowance', the position could perhaps be met by payments of 1/- a week through the Petty Cash Imprest, which seems an appropriate channel, and claimed as Office Expenses.

This was approved on 9 February.

The Second World War broke out on 1 September 1939.

16 October 1939
G.P.O. Accommodation, Z.A.54, Registry, Harrogate
to the Registrar

Traces of rats and mice have been observed at Z.A.54
during recent weeks, but it is understood that the nuisance
is kept to a minimum by the activities of a cat [called
Peter] which is a particularly efficient mouser.

The ownership of the animal is doubtful, and in any
case, after several attempts to find it a home, it has
always returned to its old haunts.

The cat is living on the vermin it catches, supplemented
by milk, etc. purchased by the caretaking staff, and it is
recommended that authority be sought to refund these
out of pocket expenses up to a maximum of one shilling
a week.

This allowance was granted on 18 October.

A cat was authorised in London in 1942 at Pentonville Road and in 1943 at Brixton Road and Northburgh Street, and at Luton – where Civil Defence uniforms were being devoured. With wartime rationing and shortages, the cats performed a vital role in protecting against losses of such equipment through attack by unpatriotic rodents. Civil Defence property was clearly their favourite dish of the day:

28 April 1942
Post Office Stores Department, Orchard Street,
**   London W.1**
to Personnel Department, Building and Supplies
**   Branch**

As a check against the depredations by rats and mice of valuable stocks of woollen and cotton materials (Civil Defence materials, etc.) held by this Department at Grays Inn Road, a cat has for some time been installed at that Depot. Covering authority is now sought for a grant of

1/- a week for the maintenance of the cat from 1st March last.

Papers 66193/42 relate to a similar allowance for keeping a cat at Pentonville Road.

Authority was granted on 21 May. In 1944 similar authority was granted at the very appropriately named Rochester Mews Depot, where cats were called in after Ministry of Works vermin destroyers had apparently failed to eradicate the mice with traps and poison.

Questions in the House

Post Office Cats of the 1950s

On 3 August 1950, the Registrar reported to the Building and Supplies Branch that, after twelve years' loyal service, the Official Post Office Headquarters cat, Minnie:

... died on 16 May and payment of the allowance towards its maintenance ceased.

The new cat ... has arrived, but it has been found on enquiry that for several years a kitten of the original cat has been kept in Headquarters Building and one of the cleaners has been looking after both animals.

Since the death of its mother the 'kitten' (it is now of course fully grown) has proved its worth as a rat catcher and its retention is recommended.

If this is agreed the question of reimbursement to the cleaner at the rate of 1/6d per week for the eleven weeks during which the allowance was suspended can perhaps be given consideration.

It is proposed to dispose of the newly acquired animal (which is an experienced mouser) by transferring it to the Aldersgate Street premises, where serious complaints have been made about the presence of rats and mice, and, if this course is approved, authority is sought for the creation of a cat allowance of 1/6d at Aldersgate Street in addition to the one at Headquarters.

4 August 1950
Building and Supplies Branch
to the Accountant General's Department

The proposals are approved as far as the PAD/BSB
[Personnel and Accommodation Department, Building
and Supplies Branch] are concerned.

*However, this simple solution to the overcatting situation
did not quite work out as anticipated:*

29 December 1950
R. G. Hughes, Chief Officer, Aldersgate
to the Registrar

I have received continuous complaints from the cleaner
at Aldersgate Street regarding the unclean habits of the
cat. In addition it is a source of annoyance to the
housekeeper who informs me that it attracts other cats
to the building during the night.

   In view of these complaints I request the necessary
authority to have the cat removed by the local R.S.P.C.A.
Inspectors.

*This somewhat harsh proposal was sanctioned on 4
January 1951.*

It will be recalled (page 99) that Warwick & Leamington had received the standard 1/- a week cat allowance early in 1939, to save parcels of Cadbury's chocolate from attack by rodents. Until 1952, this was the standard rate, with 1/6d being paid in a few exceptional cases. In this year, however, Warwick & Leamington attempted to secure a massive pay-rise for their cat:

16 January 1952
Mrs. H. M. Meades, Parcel Office, Leamington Spa to the Postmaster, Warwick & Leamington

Would it be possible for you to allow us a little more money to feed the office cat?

At the moment we get 1/- a week, while the fish and milk he has cost at least 1/- a day.

Will you please see what you can do.

21 January 1952
The Head Postmaster, Warwick & Leamington to the Accountant General's Department

A weekly payment of 1/- is at present being made for feeding the office cat. This sum is now most inadequate and extra money is given privately by members of the staff.

May permission be granted, please, to increase the payment to 5/- weekly.

On 8 February, the Accountant General referred the request to the Regional Director, Midland Region.

20 February 1952
Regional Director, Buildings Branch
to the Head Postmaster, Warwick & Leamington

[You] will perhaps say whether it is the presence of rats and mice which makes it desirable that a cat should be kept on the premises.

In a similar recent case an amount of 3/6 weekly was accepted as being adequate for a supply of cat food and milk. Would such an amount meet your requirements at Leamington?

22 February 1952
The Head Postmaster, Warwick & Leamington
to the Regional Director

The cat is kept in the Parcel Office at Leamington Spa.
This sorting office is outhoused from the Head Office in
premises previously used as stabling.

The premises are infested with rats and mice, and
despite considerable expenditure by the Ministry of
Works to prevent their infiltration into the sorting office,
an average of 12 parcels weekly were damaged by the
vermin. Since the cat has been kept on the premises no
similar claims have arisen. It is thought that the amount
of 3/6d weekly will meet the reasonable requirements for
the supply of cat food and milk at this office.

3 March 1952
The Regional Director
to the Head Postmaster, Warwick & Leamington

Authority is given for weekly payment for the keep of the
cat to be increased to 3/6d.

CATS AND JUDGES

Post Office cats share a common grievance with the High Court judges – their salaries have not been increased since 1873. But whereas judges get £5,000 a year, and have indicated politely that it is no longer enough, Post Office cats have to live on eighteen pence a week and such mice as can be found on the premises. Recent research into the status of Post Office cats ... shows that they were first put on the payroll in 1868 to prevent mice causing 'serious destruction' to money orders stored at the G.P.O. in London. The first three recruits, all female, had to be kept on a shilling a week, since it was stipulated that they must not be over-fed in the interests of their mice hunting efficiency. The cats were later reported to have done their job 'exceedingly well' and eventually their pay went up to eighteen pence a week each. One wonders how their successors manage to live on it nowadays – even with the mice thrown in.

POST OFFICE CATS

... London are allowed 1s 6d each week for rations, while cats in Manchester get only 1/-. A complaint about this to P.O. H.Q. in London got this reply:
'We have no cats at present on the payroll. The Ministry of Works has a highly efficient system for dealing with vermin.'

This was, of course, quite untrue. The P.O. did have cats on the payroll, and the most efficient system the Ministry had found was, in fact, to keep cats. This public interest in the cats' rates of pay, however, led to the following important debate in the House of Commons:

Wednesday, 18 March 1953
House of Commons
Captain L. P. S. Orr, Ulster Unionist M.P. for Down South
to Sir David Gammans, Assistant Postmaster General

Captain Orr:
When was the allowance payable for the maintenance of cats in his department last raised; what is the total amount involved; what is the present rate per cat in Northern Ireland; how does this compare with the rate in London?

Sir David Gammans:
There is, I am afraid, a certain amount of industrial chaos in the Post Office cat world. Allowances vary in different places, possibly according to the alleged efficiency of the animals and other factors. It has proved impossible to organise any scheme for payment by results or output bonus. These servants of the State are moreover frequently unreliable, capricious in their duties and liable to prolonged absenteeism. My Honourable Friend has been misinformed regarding the differences between rates for cats in Northern Ireland. Except for the cats at Post Office Headquarters who got the special allowance a few years ago, presumably for prestige reasons, there has been a general wage freeze since July 1918, but there have been no complaints.

Captain Orr:

How does my Honourable Friend account for the fact that no allowances are payable for cats in Northern Ireland? Is it because the Post Offices there are more sanitary, and will he say what happens if a cat has kittens? Is there a family allowance payment?

Sir David Gammans:

There are no cats in Northern Ireland, I presume, because there are no mice in Post Office buildings. With regard to the children's allowances, I am afraid there is none. But the Head Postmasters have full discretion to give a maternity grant.

Mr Rankin:

Can the Minister tell us whether his Department provide an adequate maternity service?

Sir David Gammans:

Very adequate.

Miss Ward:

Can my Honourable Friend say whether this is one of the occasions on which equal pay prevails?

Sir David Gammans:

Equal pay has been accepted both in principle and in practice.

Captain Orr:

In view of the unsatisfactory nature of the reply, I propose to raise this matter again.

In late 1954 and early 1955, the whole question of cat allowances was discussed in an interminable series of memos between the various regional directors. It was finally decided that they should be retained and that the authority to pay them should be granted to Head Postmasters and Telephone Managers. This ruling was approved on 10 January 1956 and incorporated into the Head Postmasters' Manual *in February 1956:*

February 1956: Revision to *Head Postmasters' Manual*

§***34B: Cat allowances.** There may be occasions when a cat on the premises may prove effective in keeping down rodents. Head Postmasters and Telephone Managers may authorise the payment of an allowance of 1/6d a week for the upkeep of a cat in such cases.

By 1956, in fact, as the price of Kit-e-Kat was now a staggering 9d (less than 4p) a tin, and a pint of milk 7½d (3p), the allowance was generally increased to 2/6d a week, and by 1958 to 3/6d a week.

*The overpaid and overfed Warwick & Leamington cat
was the subject of yet more official letters in 1957:*

1 October 1957
D. Sanders, Temporary Postwoman
to the Head Postmaster, Warwick & Leamington

I would like to point out that with the rising cost of
foodstuffs the 3/6d per week allowance for the keep of the
Official Cat is insufficient.

At the moment it is costing me almost twice that sum,
and in the circumstances I would be very grateful if an
increase could be granted, as the allowance now in force
has remained unchanged for several years.

4 October 1957
The Head Postmaster, Warwick & Leamington
to the Accountant General

Office Cat
In view of the general increase in cost of living prices perhaps the attached claim may be considered please. As far as
can be estimated the present allowance of 3/6d has been in
force for five or six years. The original allowance was 1/-
weekly. It is confirmed that no difficulty is experienced
in any part of the Office by the infestation of rats or mice.

6 October 1957
The Accountant General
to the Regional Director, Midland Region

In 1939 authority was given for the allowance of 1/- a
week for the maintenance of a cat at Warwick &

Leamington Head Post Office. It would appear, however, that for the past five or six years the sum of 3/6d a week has been paid for this purpose, and it is assumed that your general authority under SBB Directives, Chapter VII, Section C, Item 22, was obtained before this step was taken.

In 1955 – when the question of cat allowances was reviewed – it was agreed that they should be continued under certain circumstances and authority to pay such allowances was devolved on Head Postmasters and Telephone Managers. HPM RI, III.34(B) was amplified to this effect and the allowance was fixed at 1/6d a week. This amount is now under review.

In the above circumstances it is not proposed to disturb the present arrangement at Warwick and Leamington H.P.O., but it is regretted that the allowance cannot be increased above 3/6d a week. Please inform the Head Postmaster accordingly...

11 December 1957
The Regional Director, Midland Region
to the Head Postmaster, Warwick & Leamington

... note that the allowance cannot be increased. There being no record in this Branch of authority being given for the increase in the allowance from 1/- to 3/6d. Was the authority given by you?

13 December 1957
The Head Postmaster, Warwick & Leamington
to the Regional Director

Read and noted. It has been found that the papers dated March 1952 containing Regional authority for the increase in the allowance to 3/6d a week were filed at this office, and these are now enclosed.

8 January 1958
The Regional Director
to the Accountant General

It is confirmed that the allowance was increased from 1/- to 3/6d under SBB Directives, Chapter VII, Section C, Item 22. It has been noted that the present allowance cannot be increased.

10 January 1958
The Accountant General
to the Regional Director

Noted.

'Tibs the Great'

The Post Office Headquarters Hero

By the late 1950s, authority for granting cat allowances having been delegated to Postmasters, the exchanges of letters that comprise the preceding pages virtually ceased. However, it would not be possible to conclude the story of the Post Office cats without reference to Tibs, perhaps the greatest of them all.

Tibs was the offspring of Fluffy (who was probably Minnie's kitten referred to in the 3 August 1950 letter on page 104). He was born in November 1950, and presumably soon took over from Fluffy, serving at Post Office Headquarters, St. Martin's-le-Grand, London E.C.1. A giant weighing 23lbs, he lived in the St. Martin's Refreshment Club in the basement of the building. Tibs was paid 2/6d a week and was not only adored by Post Office workers but was also befriended by students and staff at nearby St. Bartholomew's Hospital. As well as keeping Post Office Headquarters completely mouse-free, his eventful fourteen-year service included an appearance at a 'Cats and Film Stars' party and his portrait appeared in a book, Cockney Cats, *by Warren Stanley Tute and Felix Fonteyn (London: Museum Press, 1953). This was an unusual pictorial survey of cats 'employed' in various London establishments. The authors recalled that Tibs was '. . . one of the larger and fiercer and better-fed cats which*

In lbs

23

we had yet come to interview'. He clearly proved a troublesome sitter, and plans to photograph him in Sir Rowland Hill's chair and greeting the uniformed doorkeeper had to be abandoned. He was coaxed instead into an 1856 pillar box, an unconventional location he decided was not sufficiently dignified, and he occupied it only long enough for a single picture to be taken before he hurtled away to resume his official duties.

Tibs' welfare was a major source of interest to all, as correspondence relating to his illness in 1957 shows:

8 March 1957
Official Bulletin

It was reported this morning that the Official Cat, Tibs, had developed an ear swelling and apparently was suffering much pain. All efforts to induce it to enter a container for transport to a veterinary centre failed.

By agreement with the Staff Duty, the People's Dispensary for Sick Animals, 169 York Way, N.7 was phoned. The P.D.S.A. representative proposed that their van should call at Headquarters Building and collect the cat for treatment at the Ilford Sanatorium and retention until recovery – expected to be about a week.

The cat was duly collected; as necessary intermediate medical treatment would not be available on official premises during week-end closure, this was the only solution.

The alacrity with which our request for treatment has been met by the voluntary organisation is very praiseworthy and it is suggested that the Department may wish to make a donation for a service of mercy so willingly given without any charge...

A P.D.S.A. collection box was duly placed in the St. Martin's Refreshment Club and over £50 raised from staff contributions.

14 May 1957
Official Report on Tibs' condition by H. A. J. Logan, Personnel Department

The condition of this cat was reported to me about midday on Friday, 8 March. It was obvious that the animal, suffering from an abscess behind the ear, could not be left in the building over the weekend and that veterinary attention had to be obtained quickly.

The first suggestions from the people concerned with the cat were that it should be taken to a veterinary surgeon (the nearest one seems to be at the Angel,

Islington), but, apart from the veterinary fee, that course would have been expensive and difficult, for the cat is such an enormous animal that it could hardly have been accepted on public transport and taxi fares would have been incurred – if taxis could have been obtained.

The P.D.S.A. were appealed to and that organisation immediately sent a van to collect the cat, kept it for nearly five weeks and cured the ear condition, and finally delivered it back to Headquarters fit and well.

No charge has been made for these services and it is understood that any payment is left to the generosity of those responsible for the animal. Although mindful of the need for economy, it seems to me that the Post Office could hardly do less than send a payment of 2 guineas, and payment of that amount is suggested...

£2.2s.0d was accordingly sent.

Tibs died 23 November 1964, and was the subject of an obituary in the January 1965 Post Office Magazine, *under the headline 'Tibs the Great is No More'. Alf Talbut, a cleaner who had looked after him throughout his life, commented, 'There will never be another Tibs.'*

P.S.

Tailpieces

Since the 1960s, Post Office cats have continued to serve quietly, but have occasionally been in the news:

In an account of 1968 there was Persil, a Manchester cat who, as he grew old, took the lift between floors when he patrolled his Post Office, and Chippy of Bridgwater who often stowed away on Taunton-bound railway vans and had to be retrieved by his keeper.

Mack, a cat at the Post Office at Bletchley, became famous overnight in 1971 when his allowance was raised from 3/6d to 10/– a week. The same newspaper report also claimed that there were once over 25,000 Post Office cats!

A report in June 1976 described Susie, a cat at Bethnal Green, London, sorting office. She had been employed for a year: 'The mice were driving us mad,' a spokesman declared, 'but since Susie arrived we have had virtually no trouble. She is worth every penny.' In the same year, Clarence, a fictitious Post Office cat, became the subject of an award-winning children's book, *The Post Office Cat* by Gail E. Haley (London: Methuen, 1976).

The *Daily Star* of 2 June 1980 reported that Wally, a female at the Bath sorting office during the previous six years, was paid £1.30 a week, while Kojak – who was paid £1.80 a week for his work at the Post Office garage near Covent Garden – was praised for his prowess by Bill Woodford, the officer in charge, who commented: 'Most weeks he manages to leave a couple of rats on my desk as well as an array of mice.' The same report contained a reference to the fact that the Cats Protection League was setting up a trade union, 'Cats in Industry' –

presumably to safeguard their rights in the event of a wildcat strike.

The London *Standard* of 11 August 1981 described Tammy, a female employed for eighteen months at Mount Pleasant sorting office, with a £1.00 a week allowance. The Union of Communications workers was quoted as commenting: 'We don't have a policy on either the remuneration of cats, or on the claims of members who spend money on them. If they are prepared to look after the interests of this cat, it's another example of their tremendous charity.' Three other London Post Office cats – at Bethnal Green, Nine Elms and the North Western District Office – were also noted. A Post Office spokesman remarked: 'Really the cats are a bit of an anachronism nowadays because instead of canvas bags we use a plastic derivative. But postmen are terribly soft-hearted and they are very well kept.'

Then there was Blackie of Post Office Headquarters – the heir to Tibs's job. On 29 June 1983 Personnel Manager John Roxby fought for a pay rise for Blackie, bringing the average cat's earnings to £2 a week, or forty times the old 'shilling a week' rate. Blackie's celebrated hundred per cent increase led to an appearance on BBC Television's 'Nationwide'.

As this book was going to press, a check round Britain's Post Offices revealed that cats are still widely employed. A detailed cat report from Scotland (which is otherwise strangely neglected in the Post Office Cat Archives) offers the following information:

Cheeky has lived at the Bag Switching Depot in Bonnington Road Lane, Edinburgh, for the past seven years. She just walked into the office one day and the workforce adopted her. She now receives an official allowance of around £4 per month for food.

Trixie and *Daisy* were both strays, but are now looked after by cleaning staff at Glasgow Head Post Office at 1–5 George Square, where they live in the basement. Trixie has been there for about ten years and Daisy for seven. Six years ago, Daisy lost an eye in an accident (nobody knows what happened) and the Head Postmaster paid for her to have an operation. The cats get paid £4.50 a month for food.

Corky was born in the former parcel office in Waterloo Street, Glasgow, about eight years ago. Her mother and three kittens were found in a mail bag brought into the office. The kittens were given away, but she gave birth again and Corky was one of a litter of four to remain at the office. She became an Official Cat five years ago and was taken with the staff to the new Parcel Concentration Office when it opened in Glasgow almost three years ago. She now lives there and is looked after by the postmen and cleaning staff. She receives an official allowance of around £4 a month.

With these latterday inheritors of over a century of tradition and stalwart service, the story of the employment of cats in the British Postal Service continues today. Somewhere in Great Britain, there will always be a Post Office cat.

Acknowledgements

Special thanks are due to Jean Farrugia and Sid Bowen of the Post Office Archives for all their patient assistance, to Malcolm Ross, Post Office Press Officer, and Shelley Neale of *Courier*. I should also like to thank my cat-loving publisher, Colin Webb, for having the recklessness to commission what is, by any standards, a bizarre book; my editor, Steve Dobell, for his inspired suggestions, and Kevin Maddison for his inimitable illustrations. Finally, the biggest thanks of all to the Post Office cats, without whom this book would never have been compiled.